# Positioning for

# Success

*Insights for startups and small business -
From a master entrepreneur*

New, expanded second edition

# Dave Berkus

Published by David Berkus DBA The Berkus Press

For corrections, company/title updates, comments, or any other inquiries, please e-mail DBerkus@berkus.com

Second Printing 2014
10 9 8 7 6 5 4 3 2

ISBN 978-1-105-04067-2

The content within this book has been previously published within the books, BERKONOMICS, and ADVANCED BERKONOMICS. Individual insights from this book are published periodically in Dave's emails and blog, www.berkonomics.com.

**Groups may order copies of the book at a group discount by contacting Dave Berkus at 626-355-5375, or at dberkus@berkus.com .**

Throughout this book, the Cambria type font was used for headlines, and text was set using the Calibri font.

The views expressed by the individuals in this book do not necessarily reflect the views shared by the companies they are employed by (or the companies mentioned in) this book. The employment status and affiliations of author with the companies referenced are subject to change.

# Contents

# INTRODUCTION

This book is the third in a series of eight short, easy to read books that guide an entrepreneur through the stages of creation, management, growth, and ultimately sale of a small business enterprise. And this is the second edition of this book, packed with half again as much materials the first edition, published in 2011.

Each section is an insight into another facet of starting a business that is not taught in business school or available in business texts, but rather the result of over fifty years of entrepreneurial experience with my own entrepreneurial companies and serving as investor, coach, mentor and board member for over forty entrepreneurial startups over the years.

Originally published as portions of three books, BASIC BERKONOMICS, BERKONOMCS, and ADVANCED BERKONOMICS, comments from entrepreneurs and professional managers after reading those books led to suggestions that I create separate mini-books for each stage of the business, to appeal to the interests of those at that stage of development, ready to absorb and implement insights that apply directly to the current stage of their business. Make them inexpensive and available as eBooks, they suggested, so that entire teams of managers could use the book as a planning tool and discussion prompt for the team in meetings.

And so this series of Small Business Success Books was born to address an opportunity. You can pick up this book and immediately relate to the insights, issues, opportunities, and exercises in this book right at the earliest stages of creating your business. This is not a replacement for "how to" books, courses, and consultants. It is a deeper opportunity to evaluate, plan, and execute strategies for growth based upon these insights that augment and amplify the usual "how to" materials available to entrepreneurs.

In this book, I'll tell personal stories from my fifty-plus years of entrepreneurial experience. But every one of us has a story to add to this mix, one of passionate entrepreneurism, sometimes inside an existing larger corporation, sometimes alone on a kitchen table, or back room desk. And it is a sure thing that many of us will have cogent, insightful additions to this caldron, culled from their own experiences. There's a place for these in the blog, www.berkonomics.com, and I welcome any and all for others to read and learn.

*Dave Berkus*

*Arcadia, California*

# Positioning for Success

This is a new world for product development, marketing and demand creation. With all the noise created by small businesses able to look and act like their big business competitors, the message you give to your potential customers is now much different than ever before. Attention spans have reduced as the amount of information bombarding us all has increased.

The resulting need is to create a strategy to better define and market your message. These insights will explore the strategic aspects of positioning, a most important element in the growth of the enterprise.

# The three legged stool of marketing excellence

Marketing is a science devised to help drive customers to your door. There are lots of ways to define how to market well, including the four P's of marketing (1): *product, price, promotion and place.* This is considered to be the producer-oriented model. These are still the driving focus behind most marketing courses, and deserve to be so.

Then there is the four C's, the consumer-oriented marketing model (2). The four Cs: *Consumer, cost, communication and convenience.* This makes sense too, and surely deserves time.

Oh boy. Then there's the compass or cardinal definitions model for marketers: *N=needs, W=wants, S=security, and E=education.* We can go on forever. But I have my own model that is even simpler.

I'll call it my IDC model, just to fit into the scheme of the conversation.

*I= increase revenues.* Find a way to position the company and the product to be wanted so much that it moves into the needs column for the consumer. Use all the techniques you learn in marketing classes to drive demand. Higher demand results in higher prices - if there is limited supply. Or, with or without limits on supply, higher demand results in greater revenues, satisfying the "I" in the formula.

*D=Decrease costs.* With greater demand comes the option to increase production and gain efficiencies of scale, driving costs down in the process. Even without higher demand, reducing costs should always be a focus for management to provide breathing room for increased profits.

And finally: *C=Customers, and more customers.* Marketing should provide a pool of ready to listen customers, no matter what the price or complexity of the product. More importantly for management, finding a way to focus on extreme customer service will be the most inexpensive, effective marketing tool of all. Existing customers have low acquisition costs, addressing the "D" in the equation. Extremely happy existing customers are the greatest marketers you will ever have.

*Increase revenues, decrease costs, and better serve customers.* IDC: that could be a motto or even a manifesto for any good management team. And it's a good place to start a focus upon positioning.

*(1) First proposed by Jerome McCarthy in 1960*
*(2) Robert Lauterborn, 1993*

# The LALA School of marketing

While we are at it, let's focus not upon the process of marketing and positioning, but on you. How should you become the best marketer you can be, even if you are a first time entrepreneur or a seasoned CEO?

There's an answer for that. The title of this insight helps us find a formula: LALA.

*Listen!* The first rule of marketing and positioning is to listen to the marketplace. Interview potential customers, hold focus groups, meet with existing customers. Hire consultants. Attend trade show education sessions. Ask you field representatives to debrief you about what they are hearing. But listen!

*Adapt!* Create, change, throw out, tweak or put more resources behind those efforts or campaigns that are working. Listening does no good without action. And the first thing in marketing is to adapt your product or service to the needs of the marketplace.

*Learn!* Measure the results of your changed program in as many ways as possible. Create metrics for customer acquisition, retention, conversion, reach, or anything that helps you to better understand the effects of your changes to the program.

*Adapt* (again)!   It's not unfair to reinforce the cycle by again adapting to the market after learning from your changes.  Start the cycle all over again, and never stop.

LALA: Listen, adapt, learn, adapt.

## Do you really want to be the first to market?

Over the years, as I managed my several computer companies as CEO or executive chairman, I made the decision to go to market with a brand new product that had never before been exposed to my customer's marketplace.  In each case, after overwhelming publicity, certainly noticed by a great number of potential decision makers, and after record-breaking sessions at industry trade shows to introduce these to the potential buyers, the products failed in the marketplace.

I recall the introduction of artificial intelligence into the hotel reservation process, a "one-up" on the airline method of yield managing the price of airplane seats.  With the cover story in the industry trade journal, record-breaking overflow education sessions at the international trade show, and even glowing reports from the first hotel user's management, the product failed to attract more than two customers and had to be withdrawn from the market, even though it was an unqualified success for the first users.  As a side note, we returned to market with the application as a software-only product without artificial intelligence and without some features, reduced the price from $150,000 to $8,000, and had a subsequent hit on our hands.

In another instance, we introduced the first kiosks for hotel lobby check-in.  They were large, a bit clumsy looking, and gathered cobwebs in the lobbies of some great hotels.

These and other efforts to be first over the years have led me to ask my current crop of CEOs as I serve on various boards, "Do you have the resources to evangelize the market, educate your potential customers,

AND sell your product?" The answer is invariably 'no,' because the cost of evangelizing a new product is completely unknown. A marketing professional or the marketing department certainly can work to obtain good press, appealing to curious journalists and early adapters. Early meetings with potential customers will yield enthusiasm for a "free test" of the new product. But if it is a radical departure from the comfort zone, the cost of promoting and marketing the new product will be beyond the capability of most small or medium sized companies.

Even Apple rarely attempts this, with all its resources. Apple is well known for building upon the work of early adapters. After failing with its early Newton tablet, Apple waited for fifteen years before reinventing and repositioning the tablet as a much friendlier consumer device. The same occurred with the iPod. Apple was not first or second. They just added the infrastructure needed to seamlessly purchase and download content to their offering, and produced a friendly way to use a product that previously required early adapters to manually download songs to their devices.

I will readily admit that the half million I spent on the artificial intelligence system that failed generated the greatest positive press we ever had. As a corporate promotion, it was a hit. As a product marketing effort, it was a failure.

If you are going to be first in a market, plan on a very long time from introduction to acceptance. Triple the time you estimate for the effort, and add four times the cost you estimated for marketing.

Does anyone know how much Toshiba lost with its HD DVD format marketing effort? First to market over blue ray with what some say was a better product, Toshiba dropped over a billion dollars into that one and lost it all. There are numerous examples like that one.

You might be an exception. Chances are that you'd do much better by inventing a better mouse trap, and marketing it for its advantages over a product that the consumer already understands. But there is always a winner at a table with the odds stacked against the player. It just doesn't happen often enough to expect success.

# The "drop dead" question for a customer survey

Sean Ellis, the marketing guru behind DropBox and other successes, advises clients that "The most important question on a survey is, 'How would you feel if you could no longer use this product?'" He goes on to quantify the response. If more than forty percent of the respondents say they would be "very disappointed," the product should go viral and be a great success. Conversely, if less than ten percent say this, those companies or products would have a hard time getting traction in the marketplace.

What a great test. It reminds us that our customers, especially early adapters, must want to continue to use our products to the extent that they "would be very disappointed" if unable to do so in the future.

What other questions could we wrap around this critical one to form a great survey that is both short enough and powerful enough to be relevant to our marketing effort, let along our R&D and production efforts?

Using Sean again as a source, we might ask: "How did you discover our company?" and provide several checkbox answers, including 'friend or colleague.' Again, it is a sign of a viral marketing effort to get more than forty percent checking that box. Then "Have you recommended our company to anyone?" Use just 'yes' and 'no' as possible answers, and look for more than fifty percent 'yes' responses.

And there is always the great open door question: "Would it be OK if we followed up by email to request a clarification to one or more of your responses?" If more than fifty percent say "yes" you have a real hit on your hands. It means you can use this respondent as a resource for case studies and marketing quotes in the future.

Keep your survey very short to insure a large number of responses. But do include at least one specific question about your product to be sure the respondent is an actual customer.

## Use video whenever possible.

Ninety percent of all traffic on the Internet is in video form. Yes, most of that is from NetFlix and YouTube and others delivering entertainment content. But an increasing amount is now coming from web sites and YouTube videos created by companies looking for an edge in their marketing efforts. The average time spent on a static website, one without videos linked to the home page, is under a minute. That time more than triples when videos are positioned to be delivered with just a home page click.

Videos are no longer expensive to produce, even though a poor amateur effort may be much worse than none at all. One way to create great company videos inexpensively is to contact your local college or university and ask if there are interns signed up for such work with local companies. Another is to combine clips you've accumulated into a professionally edited video without creating any new shots.

Each video, especially those on the front page of a site, must be compelling, to the point, and short. If you are selling a product, a one to two minute demo that is well edited will work wonders for viewer retention. If you are promoting the corporation as opposed to the product, short clips of the company's previous projects with comments from enthusiastic customers would be appropriate.

Finally, content does not last forever. Videos should be replaced or rotated at least annually to be effective over time. No matter how many videos you have to offer on your site and on your YouTube channel, videos will increase your marketing awareness.

# Only those in the fight can win.

Entrepreneurism is all about risk. Sometimes, you can reduce your personal risk by taking in other people's money, starting with a contract from a customer, purchasing a going business, or spinning off an existing revenue-generating portion of an existing business.

Even then, the risks of having enough cash to fund daily operations or growth can be daunting. The same is true about marketing. If you don't directly engage the potential customer at the right time, place and mood, you are at a disadvantage from the start. There are too many competitors for a customer's time and money to make an error in your approach and offer.

But the truth is in the headline. If you don't chose to enter the fight, it is impossible to win it.   And entering the fight without the proper resources usually assures defeat.  Resources such as money, experience, statistics about your target, experienced marketing and sales talent, and especially a compelling need and attractive product are all important to the ultimate success of an enterprise.

So ask yourself: Are you ready to enter the fight? Do you have the resources necessary to at least give you a chance to win? If not, what do you need to do so, and how can you get those resources?

I am often surprised at the inexperienced executive's estimates of time to breakeven for a product or a company, about the time and cost to market, about the expense in overhead needed to stay in the game. Most of all, I am surprised at that typical person's inexperience in the marketing arena, and understanding of the importance of marketing to the success of the product.

You may have all the other ingredients. But without an excellent marketing plan and a way to execute upon that plan, the best product and the most cash reserves won't bring in the customers. Since great marketing means addressing the wants and needs of the customer, about distancing the product from any competitor, about getting the message out to the most people possible, you've got to commit resources and energy to the fight in order to have a chance to win it.

## Use "switching costs" to your marketing advantage.

Know the cost to move from your existing platform, and estimate the switching costs for moving from a competitor's product or service to yours. Offer incentives to existing customers to stay, and for competitor's customers to switch. Protect your base with incentives to stay that are intangible - such as membership in an insider's club, access to special deals not available to others, and attention from the executives at the top.

The momentum from an old decision that took lots of effort to implement is worth something to a marketing professional. To keep an existing customer, even if by offering discounts, is much less expensive than the cost of attracting a new one. To reduce switching cost from a competitor is to lower the barriers to a quick decision that might have been otherwise much harder to make.

Increase the barriers to your customer's switching, not just with excellent service, but with some form of personal touch. Recognizing a longstanding customer with an appropriate gesture from the top is best of all.

Recently, I received a hand-written letter from two co-CEOs of a company I had helped out with a few hours of time. They accompanied the letter with a customized gift of their product that contained the logo and name of the college where they knew I was a trustee.

First, I have not received a hand-written letter other than a greeting card from any business associate in what feels like decades. I was in such shock, I did not respond in kind. What should I do? Pull out a piece of stationery that had been sitting unused for over a decade and write in longhand? You aren't supposed to respond using a less personal vehicle than the original one. So email was out. A phone call might have done it, but not with the elegance of the original correspondence. Now, every time I turn from my desk to the credenza behind, I see that letter and gift. I am not willing to just file the letter or put the gift on the shelf. That's the power of a great outreach from the top.

And that's a lesson for all of us in marketing. Find the right way to reach existing customers that stands out from the usual. Find an offer that makes switching easy for others. Pay attention to opportunities to differentiate yourself from the rest.

Someday I will file the letter and put away the customized gift. In the meantime, those two guys got many more miles from a relatively simple gesture than I would have thought possible.

## Embrace the right to pivot!

Plans don't often work as devised. We are not always smart about the market or the product. Great teams are not bound by their original product or marketing plan. Greatness finds one definition in management's ability to "pivot," or change the plan in reaction to its early response from the marketplace.

Investors celebrate teams that quickly find the flaws in the original plan and reallocate resources in another direction before more wasted effort. Even the term, pivot, seems to call up images of a light-footed dancer able to move so very quickly in any direction.

My favorite example of a world class pivot comes from the CEO and board of one of my most successful investments. Green Dot Corporation was formed by an entrepreneur in the year 2000 to create a product to permit those without credit cards to purchase items on the

Internet. Think of it: to shop on the web, you must have a card, not a nine digit routing and bank account number. The young, inexperienced entrepreneur had two assets that attracted me – rights to use the MasterCard name on this new product, and a laser focus to make this work in any form possible.

Over the years, that vision changed dramatically several times as the world's first debit cards were invented by the firm, positioning the card to be used by the un-bankable, those unable to obtain credit cards or in some cases even checking accounts. The firm grew to dominate its new field, create an infrastructure to allow any of its 70,000 retail stores to simple activate or load the card with money from any cash register. It replaced Western Union as the preferred way to send money across great distances. And it built a billion dollar market and then some - where it might have been restricted to a small percentage of that.

And we who held early stock celebrated together the ringing of the NYSE opening bell the day that often pivoting company went public.

## Lighting the match – going viral

It doesn't happen by accident. Not every new game site is a Club Penguin. Not every social network is a Facebook. Not every texting application is a Twitter.

What are the elements needed to focus upon in making the attempt to take a product viral? Intrigued by the thought, I recently made a list. It was as much in reaction to my getting blank stares from entrepreneurs when I asked that question as it was for me to better understand the problem itself. Here is my list.

First: *Planning*. Retail or end user web sites do not even receive limited notice without being discovered through a real marketing program, aimed at finding the flywheel effect (the moment of going viral that makes all the difference between failure and success.) In today's world of social marketing, it takes someone knowledgeable if not expert in understanding how to use available resources in promotion and marketing.

Second: *channels*. I am chairman of a company that distributes its product through over one hundred fifty retail Internet travel channels, all websites where someone else spent the money attracting their users and attempting to go viral. We could not have begun to reach a fraction of that audience with any amount of money if we did not reach through these channels. Sometimes, it is just the right idea to brand your product inside that of a known presence.

Third: *cost*. Even a great marketing plan to gain an audience fails if there is not enough money to prime the pump. And of course sometimes that requires a large amount, far beyond the capability of small companies looking for its initial audience.

Fourth: *measurement*. If you can't measure the results of your attempts to gain a viral response, how can you know when to focus upon reinforcing or changing the effort? Well-tuned metrics are an absolute must. And the tools for most are available, sometimes free, for the educated marketer.

Fifth: *reaction*. If everything goes right in finding the right plan, channel, cost and measure of success, and if you do nothing to reinforce the success or change the focus, the rest of the effort can easily die a slow death.

And sixth: *the pivot*. A reaction is not often enough. Many times, it takes an intelligent repositioning of the entire offering to try again from the start with revised ideas based upon learned experience.

It's a cycle that must be learned and followed in order to successfully maximize an opportunity in any industry and for any company. So, where in that cycle are you today?

## Market knowledge comes first.

*Know your market and competition, or don't spend a dime on anything else.*

I have stated previously that I love absolutes – statements with no wiggle room for gray-area responses. Well, here is one of those, and it deals with market research first and foremost.

Let me tell you a short story at my own expense. In 1994, (I know a long time ago), I invested over a million dollars into a company whose entrepreneurs had a vision that I bought into for many reasons, not the least of which was that I had industry experience and understood the need. The first of a number of advanced products was a unique cell phone for hotel rooms, connected through a special "switch" in the hotel's telephone room that was able to detect when a call was coming to the guest room phone and simultaneously ring the cell phone assigned to that room, no matter where it was at the moment. A tent card beside the fully-charged phone greeted the guest entering the room for the first time, inviting the guest to pocket the cell phone for the duration of his stay. The phone could be used for receiving incoming calls when in the restaurant, on the golf course or anywhere. The guest could even make room-to-room or concierge calls as if dialing from the room itself. These systems were not cheap as you might guess. But four and five star hotels loved the concept, which included redirecting outgoing calls from the cell phone by the guest to be sent through the hotel's land line switch, making the hotel a miniature phone company with its attendant profits.

Here's where some intelligent market research might have saved the company and my investment. Fast forward several years to 1996. Hotels were installing the system; guests were satisfied and the company was growing. There was even talk of some phone companies using the patented system for serving communities of guests, not just from a single hotel. Back to 1996. That year, some of you will recall, the first digital cell phones were released to the market, smaller, cheaper and priced with roaming plans that made it no premium cost to carry these digital phones to cities far from home. Overnight, guest use of the room cell phones dried up and hotels were left with expensive switches, phones and chargers unused. Soon the company was drifting toward bankruptcy as the leases for the systems expired, one by one.

I guarantee that there were tens of thousands of people in the country who knew long beforehand of the imminent arrival of the digital cell phone and could predict its effect upon usage, especially roaming use. And yet the company was blindsided as it continued to invest in switch and specialized analog phone hardware, soon to be instantly obsolete. Merely adapting the switches to new digital phones would not work, since guests no longer needed the service itself, being instantly self-sufficient. People no longer called guests in their rooms but directly to their cell phones, even when the guests were on the road.

In this case, the competition was not from a company but a new technology. In most cases, it is the competitor with a better product, lower price, faster service, better reputation that is the threat.

When I listen to a pitch from an enthusiastic entrepreneur or read the summary of a business plan, one of the first questions I ask is about the strength of the competition. Surprisingly, many entrepreneurs immediately respond. "There is no competition." Now, there is a statement even Alexander Graham Bell could not make about the telephone (which he pitched to his investors as a device to aid the deaf). Bell's competition was the written message, doing nothing, the telegraph and old fashioned word of mouth. To say "there is no competition" is always the most red of all flags to an investor. For most brilliant new ideas and business plans, the competition is merely to do nothing. That response is quite different than one where competitors have paved the way and existing customers prove through use that the product or service is valued.

So I lost over a million for lack of market research. Bell was lucky, but the pace of technology was so much slower then. Just to make a well-earned point now that you have heard my story, know your market and competition or don't spend a dime on anything else. Oh, how I wish I had taken my own advice.

# Find your "teacher customer."

*Your customers know what they want more than you do. Find one to teach you.*

This insight came from personal experience and from a good friend who advanced the notion of the "teacher-customer" years ago. I internalized this phrase, recalling the many times I had partnered with customers to design new feature-functionality into my hotel computer system back when such systems were brand new to the industry. It was an ideal partnership between my growing company, as it approached one hundred employees on the way to almost two hundred fifty, and selected special customers anxious and willing to spend time telling us of their pain points. Together we would work out solutions in the form of new functions, new controls, new reports, and new safeguards. The customer would be the first to receive the new functionality in a new release. At the annual user conference, I would often make sure the entire user community present knew of these extraordinary collaborations by naming the teacher-customers in the presence of their contemporaries. Sometimes the audience would cheer one of their own, knowing that everyone benefited from the extra time and effort spent teaching their vendor the needs of the industry not yet addressed by competitors or by our firm to date.

This is not to bend this insight into a claim that a company should wait to develop new, groundbreaking products and services until a customer asks for them. If that were the ideal mode, many game-changing concepts would never have made it to market, including Fred Smith's FedEx, first explained to a college professor in a paper returned with a C+ grade and the professorial comment that the idea was "good but impractical".

Even if you are an expert in an industry segment, partnering with one of those rare, willing teacher-customers during the design stage for your proposed product or service is empowering and fruitful for both parties.

All companies whether service or product-oriented must fight to gain and maintain quality of product, or fall to the bottom of the competitive heap. We have explored feature-functionality. Now it is time to focus upon stage four in our exploration of insights, product quality and its effects upon the organization.

## Don't rest until you test.

So you have a great new product or service that you and your associates love. Early adopters should climb all over each other for a look. But what have you done to test the concept against the realities of the marketplace?   Have you developed a prototype, alternate pricing schemes, even a PowerPoint mockup to show to potential buyers? I would be very, very nervous without testing the product in the market as early as possible, ready to make changes and enhancements before committing to production and release.

Even with a perfect product, is the market ready for this? Will you have to be both the evangelist for the product and for its marketplace as well? Few early stage companies have the resources to do both.

There are formal focus group organizations to help you, or you can attempt to test the market yourself by calling together a variety of potential users and asking a third party to facilitate a meeting where the product is exposed to the group and a conversation freely formed allowing the participants to agree with the premise or reject the product as useless to them, all without personalities getting in the way.

No matter how you plan to test, make that plan an integral part of the development cycle, as early as possible so changes will not be costly. Do NOT rest until you test.

# Everything changes from concept to release.

You can take this as a rule, not an exception. You'll recognize the truism, *"No battle plan ever survives contact with the enemy"* first stated by German Field Marshall Helmuth Karl Bernhard Graf von Moltke in the 19th century. This variant of the "battle plan" truism is important to internalize. A product at the concept stage contains feature-functionality that customers may not want or be willing to pay for, or which just might not work well enough for release to the public.

You may recall that Microsoft planned a new file system for Vista, but pulled the file system from the product before release, and has not released the WinFS file system yet as of this writing, years later. It is interesting to note that not many of us even remember this "feature" let alone miss it.

Plan for change; sometimes at the last minute. Allow for the cost and extra time for tweaks to the product or service. Make the first release a limited, controlled one, so that changes and corrections can be made much more easily than if a general release all at once.

And how do we protect ourselves against surprises that relate to feature-functionality as opposed to product quality upon release? Early contact exposing friendly close customers to the product are critical to the development staff, marketing and even to the customer that feels closer to your enterprise as a result of the special treatment. This is not to state that the customer tests a new product before we do internally, although many of us are surely guilty of that error.

Back when I was developing early systems for the hotel industry, with the full cooperation of the owner and managers of a hotel in Tulsa, Oklahoma, I would fly in from Los Angeles on Friday evenings, install new releases that night and make fixes on the fly in a real 24 hour environment. Sunday afternoon, just about departure time for my scheduled flight, the hotel manager would drive me to the airport barely in time to make the returning flight.  My excitement in having developed so many new and "somewhat tested" features over a sleepless weekend was exceeded only by the enthusiasm of the entire hotel staff for the new and wonderful capabilities left behind after the magic weekend of non-stop programming. These trips were so common and their aftermath so predictable (a late night emergency repair call waiting for me at home upon return Sunday evening) that the hotel owner created a mantra that stuck with me and caused quite a laugh at my expense for years.  He would be sure to remind his staff, shaking my hand goodbye as I left in a hurry to catch that Sunday evening flight: "Wheels up, system down."  I am not advocating such brazen behavior today.  "Cowboy coding" is no longer common or permissible in the computer software industry, especially for enterprise systems.  But those were the days.

# Faster is sometimes more valuable than better.
### *And doing both well usually wins the day.*


This is one of those arguable insights, where both sides win. Dell is a great example of emphasis upon fast, creating a customized computer in 48 hours or less, bringing in assemblies and components just-in-time to make the assembly line. However, if Dell quality were poor and returns high, the company surely would not have survived on speed of response alone. If someone were to ask, "What is the secret sauce, Michael Dell?" Dell's response would be something like "Quality custom computers more quickly than the competition." And in this company example, both quality and speed are the critical factors in competitive advantage.

Think of McDonalds. Its reputation is based upon fast food in a minute, with quality that is acceptable but not discernibly above the competition. Or one of the instant auto service companies where an oil change is fast and inexpensive, but the number of inspection points far fewer than at a dealer location. Speed above quality. We have become a society not used to paying even a little extra for speed, but willing to pay much more for quality. How about the $14 hamburger at a restaurant, compared to fast food? We pay for the quality of product and service, happily defining our own tolerance for cost versus quality and speed.

So in planning for your niche to defend, one of the first decisions is between quality and speed. We will soon examine the entire gamut of pricing structures, but start with this one. It is fair to repeat that quality and speed together are the winners in this contest, not one alone.

## Why buy IT? Why buy MINE? Why buy NOW?

What a powerful set of three questions. These are so succinct, so well defined, so precise that everyone in sales and everyone involved in marketing must be able to answer these three questions without pause, and convincingly.    Turning these into statements instead of questions provides a framework for the sales presentation from the highest levels of collateral materials and marketing support, to the salesperson on the front line. It would pay you to work over this set of questions in a special session with sales, marketing and senior management in the room at once.  It is that important.

*Why buy IT?*  Can you, your sales people and your marketing staff answer this succinctly?  Is your product or service one that responds to a customer need, real or perceived?  This question deals with the offering in general, not yet with your version of the product.  In general, there are three types of products or services: those a customer needs, those a customer wants, and those a customer believes he does not want or need. Your marketing and sales effort must be focused entirely upon making your product solve an urgent customer need.  Sometimes, companies do this by creating demand where none existed before, such as for *Listerine* in the early days with a campaign to eliminate halitosis, the dreaded bad breath that consumers had no name for and did not think of as a need before that most successful advertising campaign. FedEx did not respond to a need for overnight package and letter delivery; it created the need with its clever advertising campaign. Car manufacturers used to make expensive annual model changes just to create a need in the minds of consumers who then viewed their present cars as obsolete. "Why buy it?"

*Why buy MINE?* Product differentiation is absolutely necessary to make a sale when there is visible competition, as there usually is in any sale. Your marketing and sales people must know how to state clearly, with as few words as possible, the reason why your product best responds to the customer's needs.  There is quite a difference between describing features, as many untrained sales people do and most engineering types almost always do, and describing benefits as a good sales person does. What the product does is less important than why the product solves the customer's problem, and how the product does so in ways obviously better than the competitor's product. This story should never be left to the sales person to make up, or each will make a different story for the purpose of a sale, not always aligned with the company's market positioning and rarely as precise and compelling as that created by professional marketers.

*Why buy NOW?* Without creating a sense of urgency, a sales person will have trouble closing the sale, allowing competitors another chance to make their case – often with the advantage of hearing the customer recount your benefits as he heard them. It is not a good place to find yourself, and is one where the odds of finally closing the sale drop considerably. Provide incentives for the sales person to use as needed to create the sense of urgency needed to push the customer over the line and commit now. Give him or her latitude for a discount up to a maximum percentage, dunning commissions by at least that percentage to make sure the tool is not used until needed. Provide a deadline after which the price will increase, the sale will end, the product will be re-allocated to another customer, or a tax credit will expire. Make the urgency clear with the sales person, so that no customer who waivers will fail to be offered something to make the sale now.

Recently, a roofing insulation sales person had my attention as he described his company's sale that would end the next Friday, and he made sure I understood that the Federal tax credit for such energy-saving home improvements would be applicable to this sale. He went on to state that the $4,500 cost would qualify for a tax credit (not merely a less-preferable tax deduction) of $3,000, or $1,500 for each of the two bundled services he offered. Something seemed very wrong to me about this credit, which I had recalled to be 30% of the actual amount paid. Because the sales person was not credible in this one area, I told him that I would check on the credit and call him a day later. Of course it took all of a minute using my search engine to figure out that he was attempting to apply his credit offer to the retail price, not the sale price, and twice for two products instead of once for the installation as a whole. I am sure other customers fell for this, but I was angry enough for this falsification of the facts that I called the sales person and not only declined, but read him the riot act in the process. *Why buy now?* Be sure there are no misrepresentations anywhere in the sales process.

## Where there's mystery, there's margin.

Here's a phrase I created in the early 1980's to describe what I clearly saw as the last chance to make high margins on the sale of computer hardware to businesses. In the day of the mainframe and then the minicomputer, margins for manufacturers exceeded 35% and dealers were granted a 35% margin as well. Even with the usual discount of 10%, the margins on hardware were high, especially when applied to prices that exceeded $30,000 per sale.

In the early eighties, IBM helped the PC become a tool of the office, and the product crossed over from use by early adopters to the mass market. Many other PC vendors flooded the market, including an uncounted number of "white box" manufacturers who created systems out of components imported from Asia. New retail channels popped up everywhere, competing for this lucrative, growing business segment. New magazines were rushed to market, thick with advertisements for computer systems and components at bargain prices. Many companies found internal employees able to install these computers and load software easily, without employing outside professional services.

And those of us depending upon the high margins from more expensive minicomputers found ourselves competing with these same PC's, now growing to be as powerful as the much more complex and expensive computers of just a few years ago.

Yet, there was one segment of the PC market that was not only growing but maintaining its margins as well as providing more professional services work than any other segment of the industry. Most of us could install a computer, but almost none of us could network that computer with others in the office or with other offices without equipment we did not understand, configuration tasks we could not perform, and training we could not offer. So we called upon our local value-added reseller with networking experience, often blessed with an earned certification by Novell or Microsoft. We paid high per-hour charges for professional services and unknowingly paid high prices for the networking equipment. But we were, as a class, happy with the fact that the computer and software costs had fallen so much that the networking costs were not an overwhelming portion of the computer budget.

Observing this, when in a planning session one day, I told my staff that we needed to find an area to defend our margins, one that still enjoyed the mantle of mystery to our customer base. Because, I said, *"Where there's mystery, there's margin."* We did find that niche and used it successfully for several years, in charging to certify and configure a company's self-purchased PC's so that they would work efficiently with our software systems. No employee of our customer company could do this because no employee knew our software and its requirements for database setup, multi-user security and more. We were able to add $1,500 or more to each small installation, and much more for large installations even though we no longer sold the PC hardware.

I told this story often in speeches to software and vertical reseller organizations, and the "mystery" expression stuck. Not only that, but I began to hear it restated back to me describing other industries in which similar progress had caused companies to search for a "secret sauce" they could defend.

It was only a small step to incorporate this into the strategic planning sessions for all companies that I later advised or served as a board member. And it still is important today.

I am an investor in a large home service company that specializes only in technology installations and repairs for the home and small business customer. With a fleet of Mini Cooper cars all marked with the distinctive logo and colors of the company, this fleet serves a growing need for fixing computer crashes, infected computers, networking issues, audio-visual installations and even fiber-optic installation in-home for a major phone-bandwidth supplier.  They discovered the niche that many home owners and small businesses could not fill or understand.

Can you find a pain point where the customer cannot apply a solution without your help?  One where the cost and value are both defensible in maintaining higher margins?

## Pick your pricing niche carefully. Defend it.

There are five major classes or niches a company should examine and make its own in calculating positioning in the marketplace.  They are:

- Price

- Quality

- Service

- Innovation

- Elegance

Companies that compete on price rarely compete against others who emphasize service or quality.  Internet resellers have a better chance to combine price and quality than those with much more fixed overhead occupying a bricks-and-mortar physical presence in the community.  But it is important for the image of the company to be known for one of the above attributes above others.

Some examples:  Wal-Mart is known for lowest prices, often for identical merchandise found in other stores for more.  But few go to Wal-Mart for quality brands, understanding that they accept Wal-Mart as the low-priced leader. Nordstrom's competes on service above all, quality second and price a distant third. We enter a Nordstrom's store expecting superior service and know we will pay a price for this. Apple charges a premium for innovative products, with quality second and service third. Mercedes offers a premium automobile with its customers expecting luxury first, quality second, service third, and price a distant fourth. If Apple released a $229 notebook computer, it would damage the brand and reduce the value of owning an Apple computer in the minds of existing customers.

The very image of a company is influenced by this decision, as is every decision following the price positioning. In many markets, there are poorly defended niches, even markets with dominant players. Asus found this in the notebook and netbook market and moved in quickly to overtake all other manufacturers with low prices. It should be noted in passing however, that competing on price alone is the most dangerous strategy of all, since other well-capitalized players can easily join the competition merely by dropping prices upon existing products, of course at the expense of its previous positioning as described above. Asus was able to grab the mantle of price king while maintaining reasonable quality and even provide a bit of innovation in the netbook arena, worthy of applause by those of us market-watchers looking for examples of good strategic price positioning.

## Plan for your 'every three million dollar crisis.'

Here is a phenomenon I discovered over time when dealing with many small start-ups in their early revenue period. A very predictable series of rotating crises seemed to befall most every one of these young companies. These became so predictable that I could accurately label them as occurring about every $3 million in gross profit (or revenue for service companies). By defining this in terms of gross profit, we can therefore include distributors with 15% gross margins as easily as software companies boasting nearly 100% gross margin.

There is a rotating series of predictable crises that most often reveal themselves like this:

At the $3 million revenue mark, the company often has grown from founders to about 20 employees, or $150 thousand in revenue (gross profit) per employee. Of course, venture-funded startups with long product creation times do not fit this mold as easily, often funded for long periods of losses with many more employees at hand in development positions. But at or around the 20 employee mark, the founders usually find that two things occur. The original management span of control is exceeded and management must be delegated to one or more middle managers to maintain efficiency in the workplace. Second, some of the original employees, occasionally one or two friends of the founders, are discovered to be falling behind as more professional employees show them up to be less competitive in their jobs. So management reorganizes the structure of the organization to fit the new needs of the growing enterprise.

At about the $6 million mark, revenues have ramped to the extent where the original product standards of quality are challenged, as is the speed and efficiency of customer service. Changes need to be made quickly to preserve the reputation of the company, adding a quality control function if not present, adding more QC steps in the process, addressing the number of customer service people on the line, creating longer hours to serve a larger customer base. Failure to respond to this predictable crisis quickly labels a company as a provider of poor quality, which seems to travel unbelievably fast among the industry, helped by competitors anxious to point out the problems. And once fixed, the perception of a fixed problem lags the reality by many months, making this a particularly tough crisis, common as it is.

At around the $9 million mark, the company suffers a most predictable cash crisis, one where the costs of growth in working capital and infrastructure creates the need for new sources of funds from investors, banks or asset-based lenders. If the company is not profitable, these channels for capital are not as easily tapped, extending the crisis and challenging the health of the enterprise.

Surprise. At around the $12 million mark, the company finds itself full circle, and in need of reorganization again along with a bit of house cleaning, pruning the poorer performers from the ranks. That's about at the 80 employee count, a time a little beyond when the company should have transitioned to a professional human resources manager to help solve this and future employee crises.

Do these sound familiar? They should, even if the dollar amounts are out of alignment with your experience, since some companies are funded well enough to skip the first financial crisis and some so efficient as to skip the first organizational crisis.

With this insight, you should be equipped to spot early signs of each crisis and plan around them in time to avoid the full impact of each in turn.

## Organize globally.

Even the smallest business can now reach throughout the globe to find resources for design, development, support and consultation. There are people and companies everywhere willing to work by the hour, providing great skill sets as needed, able to be shed when the job is complete.

Some of the best companies I have become involved with are composed of a few critical people who have relationships with a number of service suppliers around the world to add to the team as needed.

If you start out with the concept that you need only a key group of people who know how to reach out to find and manage outside resources around the globe, your chances of success with your available financial resources grows geometrically.

So why not organize from the start around such a strategy and hire those able to demonstrate those organizational skills?

# Stay current or the market will drift away.

*Markets and competitors change. Are you being left behind?*

Over the years, I have often heard the complaint from CEO friends that they have become so swamped by the demands of their growing businesses that they feel themselves further and further from the center of their industry, no longer at the forefront of information and competitive development.

It is a real risk for the successful entrepreneur that the daily demands of business make it more and more difficult to know the pulse of the industry, which becomes more and more risky as decisions are made and resources allocated to projects or products that may no longer be as attractive as before.

During the past several years, some very big bets have been made by large companies and well-healed entrepreneurs in old media, newspapers and TV stations. Although newspapers have a window in which to reinvent themselves by providing electronic delivery and TV the same by recasting into more niche markets through division of digital channels into niche-serving slices, I doubt that these bets will prove profitable in the end, because of the overwhelming availability of free media using the web. Were these companies and entrepreneurs out to a long lunch during the media transformation? Or do they know something all of us commoners do not?

## Develop the "What if" question chain method.

One of the most valuable tools in an executive's arsenal is the use of the question chain in planning meetings or to analyze scenarios that might result from an action. The powerful words are "What if..." followed by an ever-deeper question that follows the possible results of an action, or a decision based upon the last "What if" question.

The beauty of this method is that it causes the person proposing the solution to think much more deeply than during the development process, unveiling many possible consequences to be considered before implementation of an idea or project. When I use this technique, invariably the person on the other side of the question will at some point state, "I didn't think of that."

In a recent CEO roundtable, the executives discussed their experiences with the question chain. Several had revealing things to say about their experiences. One stated that he asked "what if" the U.S. dollar was to sink in value during the life of the foreign transaction. The subordinate had not thought of this carefully enough and had no protections built into the agreement or any strategies to hedge currencies. The net cost of such a failure to pre-think this event would have been in the millions, stated the CEO, but were successfully hedged against just as the dollar declined. Another CEO in the group offered his experience with the question chain relative to the availability of isotopes for his company's medical instrument customers in the event of political turmoil in the countries where the nuclear material was exported. As a result, his was the only company among the competition to continue to service his medical industry customers when just such an event occurred.

"What if" are two very powerful words when used together. Use them more frequently as you manage your enterprise.

# It is satisfying but rarely profitable serving early adopters.

I am a gadget freak, often purchasing new technologies in their first release. And my closet is full of such gadgets, from early pen-based computers to early brick-sized cell phones to an electronic handwriting recognition pad received as a gift to test. These early dives into new technologies serve a purpose for me. They keep me at the leading edge of new development as it is productized, even before mass production. They allow me to preview new devices and technologies before release so that I might write about and speak about them in my "Tech Trends" keynotes. And they are always the center of attention with my tech-savvy friends, some of whom are in the habit of asking, "So what's new today" each time we meet.

The cost of such attention-seeking and research is relatively low for me, and certainly the reward of being sought out as a speaker addressing the trends in technology is enough in itself.

But I have been on the other side of the early adopter development process several times in the past, and can attest that it is great fun, but rarely profitable to be the first with any new product that requires simultaneously evangelizing or teaching the masses within the industry and marketing the new product offering. The costs in playing such a dual role are many times that of those in positioning a new product in a niche already opened by another. And statistically, the first product into a niche is very rarely the one to succeed.

Apple, for example, was nowhere near the first to introduce an MP3 handheld music player. I had owned several before the first iPod was released. Apple learned that their leverage was in the simultaneous creation of an easy-to-use retail music store for seamlessly downloading songs, podcasts and later applications to the device. It did not hurt that Apple always seemed to trump the competition in design of the product and the product's user interface too.

In 1986, while in the hotel technology business, I observed the back-room success of American Airlines with their new Sabre subsidiary and its creation of a "yield management" system to use massive data to project demand for an airline seat on a particular flight segment days and months into the future. I was not alone among hotel industry executives curious for more information. And Sabre was not talking to anyone about their magic potion. First Hyatt Hotels, then Marriott Corporation called me to their respective headquarters to consult with their executives on this subject under a non-disclosure with each. I became even more excited about the concept applied to the hotel industry. Both of those chains had very primitive modules in their respective reservation systems. Marriott called theirs "tier pricing". If a future date was already booked at 80%, then they would eliminate any discounts below 10% from the "rack" or standard room rate. At 90% they would stop discounting entirely. These elementary steps were in the right direction but very primitive.

So I set about partnering with a small group of MIT graduates to produce specialized decision software for the hotel industry using the "LISP" programming language, created just for decision-making, allowing for coding inductive and deductive logic into the software. I partnered with Texas Instruments, producer of a LISP computer, the TI Explorer. We designed and produced special cards for the TI that would allow Apple Macintosh workstations to be used, with their handsome graphic user interface. Then I designed what was then a ground-breaking new software system that could analyze tons of data from past guest stays on the same date a year earlier and other dates with the same day of week, add factoring for city-wide events on any future date such as pro football games and conventions, analyze the speed of increase in any night's future reservations, and much more. Each night, the system was designed to perform its analysis using real advance reservations data current to the moment, and run the data through a series of rules I wrote which could be modified or added to by local hotel management, to automatically make pricing decisions and automatically implement them. The system coordinated decisions between the reservations department which accepted individual or transient reservations and the group sales department booking groups at a discounted rate, allocating available rooms between each in order to achieve maximum revenue for any future date.

I found a willing test site in the Royal Sonesta Hotel in Cambridge, Massachusetts, whose management was thrilled to participate in an industry-changing experiment with new technology. The system was priced at $150 thousand, but we calculated that the average decision implemented for the 300 room property should be worth $5 thousand, making payback within an amazing 60 days if all worked as planned. Our company installed the system, integrated it with the Sonesta computer system which our company had previously provided, trained the staff, and began to measure the results after turning on the system in a live environment. In the meantime, we sold a second system to a large timeshare resort in Orlando for the same price. By agreement, Sonesta withheld payment until completion of the beta test period.

The industry's annual technology trade show came up during these tests. The industry was abuzz about this "artificial intelligence" system and its purported early results, and I wrote the cover story for the industry magazine about the system, and organized a panel composed of executives from Sonesta, Marriott and other chains to present and discuss this newest industry marvel. On the day and hour of the panel, it became obvious that the house was way overbooked. We agreed to repeat the panel later that day for the hundreds of people unable to get into the large room. We were a great success with a great, ground-breaking product.

And the next week we asked for payment from the test property, after sign-offs from all of its managers but the top one. The general manager was also an executive of the family chain of hotels. He called me in, along with several of the second level managers so enthused about the system, and stated, "This is nice, but I could do this work on the back of a napkin," shocking us all, and he refused the pay for the machine. I challenged him immediately. "Let's disconnect the system from influencing the reservation system for one week," I offered, "and let the machine calculate but not implement its decisions. During that week, you make your decisions each night on the back of your napkin. At the end of the week, we'll compare the effectiveness of each. If you agree that our system was more likely to positively affect revenues on those dates targeted, you pay for the system. If not, we'll remove the test system and find another home for it." He agreed. Management added a few new rules to the rule base and watched over the system each evening, anxious that there be no contest between this number-crunching wonder and a single manager's intuitive guesses.

A week later, I again traveled across the country to the property to meet with the same team and the general manager. We printed out the week's decisions, those not implemented. We presented our findings, and waited for the GM's response. "I did not bother," he stated. "I have no doubt that I could have done this better if I'd taken the time; but I was busy this week."

We could not argue with the money, even if we were right and all other managers desperately wanted to keep the wonder machine. So we removed the system. After all that great press, I realized that the industry just was not ready for such a leap, giving up authority to a computer, even if at least one major airline had successfully done so. I offered to repurchase the second machine from the hotel in Florida. After all, what company can maintain such a small number of unique systems?

I turned to Tom, our chief programmer (see number 74), and directed him to use as many of the features of the knowledge based (artificial intelligence) system as possible, but reprogrammed into our standard reservations module using our BASIC programming language. Tom's team did just that, perhaps saving 70-80% of the functionality even if none of the leading edge glitz. We priced the reduced "feature" at $8,000, and sold many over the years as mere add-ins to the reservation system.

After spending over a half million on the project (and receiving at least that in great publicity), I learned a lesson repeated here. *It is satisfying but rarely profitable to cater to early adopters.*

# The four "P's" of Building a Great Business.

Some of us remember things better when given a catchy phrase or rhyme. Here's one to help you with squeezing the most out of your available resources. It reflects the new reality in our business world, one with little room for mistakes and no room for bloat within our companies.

The first "P" stands for *people*. The wrong person in a job causes all below or above that person in the production system, that depend upon that person, to operate at a reduced rate or quality of output. And if there are people depending upon the output of that wrongly-placed individual, they too will suffer from reduced resources to complete their jobs. The cost of a bad or failed placement in any position in a company's critical chain is enormous and goes far beyond the salary paid to that individual.

The second "P" is for *productivity*. If a good person is failing at the job, it may be because *you* have not provided the resources necessary for that person to do the job expected. Hire a great sales person then fail to support him or her with a good marketing effort or a properly priced quality product, and that person will be set up to fail, and for reasons you might have fixed.

Then there is the third "P" – *performance*. Like a great orchestra, it takes a skilled conductor to bring the best out of the collective members of the group. You are responsible for the quality of performance that defines an excellent enterprise and assures long life for the company as competition becomes more aggressive and geographically extended.

The fourth "P" is for *process.* How to get your offering from development to market? How to stage and tune a production line for maximum quality and output? How to penetrate an established market with a groundbreaking new product, but on a limited budget? All these are process questions, often faced by management when seeking success.

All of us have limited resources and must deploy them effectively to gain the most possible ground in the marketplace. Like a chain with four links, no one of these can be weak and allow us to succeed in our endeavor.

Focus and attention must be paid to each to strengthen the chain. Over time we will explore these issues more deeply using the "theory of constraints" (TOC) method of looking into your physical and financial roadblocks.

The four "P's": *People, productivity, performance and process.*

Which of these four P's is your weakest link? What can you do to rethink, reinforce and redirect resources and remove roadblocks to the success of that link and enhance your whole organization?

## Find your core competency.

Consider your core. It is the one skill, process or advantage you have over your competition. Then think of all the things you do to surround that core with people and assets that complete the company and allow you to release your product or perform your service.

Now consider how many of those surrounding assets and services are really necessary for you to perform in order to protect and grow your core. For most small and medium-sized businesses, there are lots of wheels spinning around the core that take up the attention and resources of management, but add little or no value to the core of the business.

These are new times, enhanced by our global ability to find resources anywhere on earth to complement the core of our business. And most often, the companies supplying those services are much more efficient at doing so than we could be because of their experience and advantages of scale, and the cost to us of such services is lower than performing them ourselves.

So – what is your core offering? Are you building it more slowly because your resources and attention are focused around many processes not critical to that core?

## Protect and grow your core competency.

It is a rule that early stage managers should find, protect and grow the core business, finding resources wherever possible to service that core in the form of variable expense, to be added to or shed at will as the company finds its niche and establishes a pattern of growth.

From administrative services supplied by personal assistants located in India, to designers and producers of prototypes in China, to call centers managed and located in the Philippines, there are efficient, well organized solutions for virtually every process needed by a company to surround its core.

In earlier college business administration courses, professors often touted the advantages of "vertical integration," the process of bringing all production from raw materials through the finished product under one roof. With the advent of worldwide seamless communication and cheaper skilled labor available through virtual relationships, that old school thinking no longer holds, even for the largest corporations capable of performing all operations in house.

Henry Ford located his auto plant near the river so that his steel mill could cool the raw product and feed the plant across the property. And in the 1960's, I created a vertically integrated record manufacturing plant where raw materials came in one door and finished record albums out the door of the same building. It was considered the most efficient possible organization at that time. But it proved impossible to shed overhead during downturns. Labor and downturn cash flow issues and management distractions contributed to offsetting the positive effects of such a practice. I doubt Ford would organize his plant that way today, and neither would I. There are far too many alternatives that serve to protect the business during downturns, give management alternatives and provide superior results when not at the core of the company's offering.

## Really do think outside the box.

Creative entrepreneurs find niches for their business that are not full of competitors fighting over the last dollar of margin, or niches that are mature and shrinking in size. They search for areas unexplored, or those covered by companies with less of a vision for quality, service or innovation.

But even creative entrepreneurs are often trapped inside the box of their experience. Recently in a discussion of this very subject in a roundtable of CEO's, one CEO reminded us of the Titanic tragedy. She stated that those in charge during the last hours aboard had options probably never considered that could have saved many more lives, given the limited number of life boats available. She listed several, including pulling up the teak floorboards and throwing them overboard along with the deck chairs and dining tables, all to be used for floatation. It made us all think that we had never considered such solutions when contemplating that disaster after the fact.

With that challenge, we turned as a group to discuss how CEO's could make a culture of thinking outside of that restrictive box of experience. We considered adding questions to the interview process that could bring surprising answers from a job candidate, pointing to a creative thinker that might complement the team.

We challenged ourselves as a group to think of answers to problems that a writer of fiction might create, unconstrained by conventional thinking. We worried over the fact that we may have hired people in the past that fit our image of the proper addition to our core staffs, people with similar experiences and training, constrained by the same experiential thinking as ourselves.

And we left that meeting each more willing to search for talent to help us and our enterprise find creative alternatives that would challenge us, expand our product, marketing, sales and process abilities beyond the constraints of our present definition of our company and its core.

## Manage your MANTRA.

I am constantly surprised when speaking with entrepreneurs and CEO's who act puzzled and a bit flustered when I ask, "So what is your mantra? Tell me about your company in ten words or less." Almost every one begins a long explanation of their business that is nearly impossible to follow, let alone recall a few moments later.

And each lost an opportunity to tell their story in a memorable way that has power and boosts their enterprise value in the minds of the listener. I recently spent fifteen minutes in front of a table-top display, attempting to coach an entrepreneur who repeatedly tried to state why his business was better than a competitor (one I didn't recognize) and never explaining what it was that he did.

In explaining what you do, and what you do better than the other company, you have seconds - and only seconds - to get your image across into the minds of your listener. The best way to do this with a young company without name recognition is to appropriate the image of another, known company, to invoke the quick mental understanding of what you do.

"We are the Skype of moderated Internet broadcasting," evokes immediately the mental picture of a company that provides a platform for broadcasting town hall meetings or large group gatherings over the Internet, much as Skype does with one-to-one video connectivity. Yet, if you took the time to describe the company with the longer description above, you'd lose many of your listeners with too much detail and too many words. With the short description evoking the image of a known company, the listener immediately grasps enough to engage in a discussion – or at least walk away and be able to repeat to another the main thrust of the business.

That's a mantra: a short, quickly understood picture of your business in just a few words, often using the name of a well-known company or process to complete the picture-story.

You have only seconds to make a first impression. Your mantra is the ticket to entrance into a longer conversation. It is often the most powerful but inexpensive marketing tool a young company has to offer. And it is often extremely difficult to craft effectively in just a few words.

So what is your mantra?

## Incremental differentiation doesn't cut it anymore.

One important element of positioning a company is pricing strategy. There are five niches you can chose when defining your positioning strategy: price, quality, service, innovation, and elegance.

And although many positioning efforts cross the lines between these, great companies play to the strength of just one. And within that slice of differentiation, to make any sort of impact and lasting company, the difference between you and your competitor cannot be incremental. "Me too" positioning is lost in the noise of today's targeted marketing and corporate reach through inexpensive, but effective, use of Internet marketing.

First, and easiest to understand, is creating differentiation by price. Certainly Wal-Mart, Target and others have gotten the attention of their potential customers using price as the primary leader to drive sales. Wal-Mart succeeds because it has changed the game with its suppliers, actually partnering with them to help drive costs down so that prices can truly be lower at the store level. Since that capability is far beyond most every other retailer, there is great risk in competing by price alone. Most anyone else can meet or beat your price any time they wish. And their motive may have little to do with short term profit, a most frustrating finding when you finally realize that it is impossible to compete with such driven opposites.

Price can become a competitive tool by creative companies when they can change the game, reducing the number of parts for example to lower manufacturing costs, or reducing the time to install a product, lowering after-sale costs. But, for the most part, competing on price alone is not a good strategy for the long run. Success is not rewarded appropriately by continued dominance of a niche when price alone built that niche.

Quality can be, and is, an important differentiator. Ford returned from the land of the nearly-dead to become not only profitable but a desirable alternative to the dominant Japanese cars by emphasizing quality at competitive prices. And some brands are built principally upon quality even at increased price, including Mercedes, Jaguar and Lincoln, to name a few auto brands that have successfully been able to charge more for quality than just the added features above their lower-priced competitors.

Service is a remarkable differentiator. Those who shop constantly at Nordstrom's are knowingly paying more for personalized service that has proved endearing and able to withstand the competition for decades of continued high standards, uncompromised by the need for profit first, service second. Internet hosting providers, iSPs, are often distinguished by larger potential customers by the level of uptime which equates to quality of service, even at incrementally higher hosting cost.

Innovation certainly defines a number of companies catering to early adopters and the mass audiences that follow. Apple stands out as the first name on most minds when thinking of innovation, even though Apple originated none of its dominant product lines, choosing instead to come to market with innovative adaptations of existing products. The iPad created an entirely new market segment from what was for over a decade a sleepy niche computer tablet market dominated by a few small-selling products aimed at niche markets.

And finally, elegance serves as a major differentiator for those who are willing to add quality and service into a brand that is priced well above reach of the masses. Coach, Bentley, Patek Philippe, and Chanel are brands defined by elegance, not feature-functionality and certainly not by being the low priced competitor. The great benefit of reaching for differentiation outside of low price is that the public you court is the public loyal to you over time because of your brand and your brand recognition, and the least likely to abandon you for another when their price is lower by increments.

Branding, price strategy, and positioning are related as differentiators that help you to increase margins and drive profits when competitors fail with inferior strategies.

## Define your story before anyone else does.

It is an old warning in the entertainment industry. Define your persona the way you want others to view you – before someone else defines you by comparing you to someone not as flattering as you would like.

I have a friend in the music business who worked hard to gain introductions to, and become mentored by, several known names in the business. One well known informal mentor called him the "Stevie Wonder of Hip Hop." That description stuck, and it is helping the young artist to define himself through instant branding and a positive image.

If you are proud of the fact that you were first to market with a product or service, you might define yourself as the "first and best". If you are the largest company in your niche, you might want to define yourself by relative size, which connotes success and staying power. If you are the quirkiest of suppliers in your niche, you could create a campaign around your company's counter culture.

One great way to define your story is with a word picture in which you associate yourself with a person or company that is recognized in a positive way and helps you tell your story more easily. For example, if you have a bicycle currier service that you want to be known as speedy and reliable, define yourself as "the FedEx of urban curriers." (See "Manage Your Mantra" earlier in this book.) Your failure to do this early in the life of the company may come back to haunt you when others refer to you as just another street currier.

How do you define yourself?  A mantra, tag line, motto, or logo with your unique brand definition is a good start.  Press releases and PowerPoint presentations with a uniform use of the mantra or phrase will reinforce your effort.  Back your story up with a statistic if possible. "There may be forty companies that do what we do, but we're the first, largest and used by more Fortune 500 companies in our area than all the others combined." (You can tell that story by limiting your market to the lower east side of town, where you are all of those things.)

Teaching your associates and employees to use the phrase each time they introduce the company to another social or business contact helps spread the word.  There is no one who will ever be as passionate about telling your story as you.  It is worth the time and effort to work on telling it well and in a memorable way.

## A good case study is worth many paid ads.

We have grown more than a bit weary of most advertising, no matter in what form.  We are constantly bombarded by ads in multiple types of media, to the extent that we most often tune them out unless particularly entertaining from the first moment.

In my keynotes on trends in technology, I often lead into one of the trends with the proposition that we have left *the information age* and are solidly within *the age of recommendation*, pointing to the fact that 69 percent of us research major purchases online before buying; 62 percent look at online peer reviews and 39 percent of us compare prices across outlets. I make the point that this is good for consumers, because it creates an environment where there is much more consumer pull - and less producer push - in our new world of connectivity and transparency.

How do you reach an audience that pays less attention to advertising then at any time in the past one hundred years?  Given the statistics quoted above, you must find ways to have your consumers endorse your product publicly, and in a form that is divorced from looking like an advertisement.

There are a number of ways to do this effectively, including the use of social networks to create buzz, seeding product acceptance through early adopters or celebrities, or by creating a small niche market that shows unusual acceptance and more. People are more trusting of unknown third parties endorsing your product that they are of direct ads touting the benefits of the product in large, clear type.

And the best way to do this is with the placement of a case study, a story told about and by a satisfied customer with something to say about how your product solved their problem or pain. That story can be in print or in multimedia form. But it must be told about and by the customer, with your product as the tool of solution, not the focus of the story. A good case study quickly lays out the pain, the players, the search, the solution, and the pain-reliving effect after implementing the solution.

All of us can identify with a successful solution to a painful problem. And some number of readers will identify directly with the problem as their own, and be moved to act. The only named solution will have been yours. And that's delivering power at the right moment to the right recipient.

Over the years, advertising money is being moved from display ads in magazines and newspapers to social network sites where people with eyeballs have migrated. But people still read, hear and see stories they can identify with, and content providers still need content. Where content providers or publishers push back when seeing a press release, many will embrace a good story demonstrating a painful problem and a happy ending. And as a result, more money is flowing into story-telling.

Particularly for companies with limited marketing budgets, case studies are perhaps the most effective marketing tool available for the cost – other than just lucky or skillfully-ignited buzz.

# Reinvent your business with bits not atoms.

If only newspaper publishers, book publishers, record companies, and movie producers would have had the vision to see their future as we now see it, we might have become a digital society with much less disruption and loss of jobs than we have experienced these past years and continue to experience.

Did the proprietor of the neighborhood bookstore or national rental chain not see this coming? Frictionless distribution through moving bits of information is so much cheaper for all but those making their living in the middle of the supply chain. Money always flows to the most inexpensive solution that meets the needs of a buyer. It should have been obvious to all in those niches and others like it that digital distribution would supplant product manufacture, inventories, physical distribution systems, warehouses, and limited retail shelf space, as soon as the infrastructure allowed it to do so.

And yet, as we have explored in past insights, it is human nature to protect the business, the existing product and the existing revenue stream - and against human nature to displace one's own product when it is still generating good income.

There are many ways businesses can reinvent themselves, even if a product must be manufactured and put into the hands of the user in physical form. Product marketing materials, user manuals, service manuals, sales guides, and catalogs all must migrate to the web to cut the use of paper and make them more accessible over time and distance. But even more important to the future of your company is the deliberate reinvention of how the essence of the company's core is delivered.

Can a consultant be as effective when half or more of the meetings held are using Skype or telepresence? Can a software product be delivered as a service "on demand," saving hardware and human error in updates? Is there a way to speed to the user a product, such as a new music release, to gain instant gratification and lesser cost at the same time?

Everywhere we look the supply chain is being disrupted by companies finding ways to deliver bits of information or entertainment instead of atoms of paper, DVDs or hardware.

In your strategic planning, do you consider ways to obsolete one or more of your products or services by delivering it in bits not atoms?

# About the author...

Dave Berkus has a proven track record in operations, venture investing and corporate board service, both public and private. As an entrepreneur, he has formed, managed and sold successful businesses in the entertainment and software arenas. As a private equity investor, he has obtained healthy returns from liquidity events in over a dozen investments in early-stage ventures. As a corporate mentor and director, he was named *"Director of the Year"* for his directorship efforts with over 40 companies in the past decade.

Dave was the founder of **Computerized Lodging Systems Inc.,** *(CLS),* which he guided as founder and CEO for over a decade that included two consecutive years on the *Inc.500* list of America's fastest growing companies, expansion to six foreign subsidiaries and twenty-nine foreign distributors, while capturing 16% of the world market for his enterprise products. Known as a hospitality industry visionary with many "firsts" to his credit and for his accomplishments in advancing technology in the hospitality industry, in 1998 he was inducted into the **Hospitality (HFTP) "International Hall of Fame,"** one of only thirty so honored worldwide over the years.

He has made over 80 investments in early stage ventures, for which he has an IRR of 97%, which includes capital contributions to his two funds (**Berkus Technology Ventures, LLC** and **Kodiak Ventures, L.P.**, for which he is the managing partner). He is also Chairman Emeritus of the Tech Coast Angels, one of the largest angel networks in the United States.

In recognition for adding significant shareholder value for emerging technology companies over the past decade, he was named **"Director of the Year-Early Stage Businesses"** by the *Forum for Corporate Directors* of Orange County, California and **"Technology Leader of the Year"** by the Los Angeles County Board of Supervisors. Dave currently sits on ten corporate boards and four non-profit boards.

Dave is also a senior partner in the twenty year old consulting firm of *Hospitality Automation Consultants, LTD (HACL)*, and lends his considerable visionary and strategic talents to worldwide hospitality chains and groups. He is the partner responsible for business process reorganization, strategic planning, software development and wide-area network infrastructure, and enterprise management systems.

A graduate of Occidental College, Dave currently serves as a Trustee of the College. Aside from this book, he is author of the first *"BERKONOMICS"* and its accompanying workbook, *"Extending the Runway"* published by Aspatore Press, and co-author of *"Better Than Money!"*- all books for emerging growth technology company executives. Dave serves as Board Member of the San Gabriel Valley Council of *Boy Scouts of America*, Board Member of the *Forum for Corporate Directors*, and is Chairman of the Advisory Board of the technology arm of the *ABL Organization*, a networking organization of CEOs in high tech businesses.

He is often engaged as keynote speaker for events worldwide, speaking on trends in technology and of legal and practical issues of governance for emerging company corporate boards.

**To contact Mr. Berkus for speaking engagements or workshops, email dberkus@berkus.com , or phone (626)355-5375.**

**Dave's books are available for purchase from the above website, or the same source from which this book was purchased.**

**Subscribe to the free weekly email or blog, www.Berkonomics.com, containing much of the information from Dave's books with lots of comments from readers with their own stories to tell.**

**Follow Dave on Twitter (@daveberkus) and Facebook (Dave.Berkus).**

**Other books by Dave Berkus available directly from *www.berkus.com* or from your favorite bookseller or online store:**

### EXTENDING THE RUNWAY
*Aspatore Press / Thompson West Publications*

The five tools board members and executives can use to help their companies succeed.   How boards and CEOs should relate to each other for growing the enterprise. Fifty-eight critical questions boards and management should consider in order to assure their mutual alignment.

### BERKONOMICS
*Hard cover, soft cover and eBook editions*

Volume one of this series. One hundred and one critical insights for entrepreneurs, CEOs and board members covering the life of the company from ignition through liquidity event.   Dave tells over fifty stories to illustrate his insights, culled from his experience as entrepreneur and service on over forty corporate and ten non-profit boards.

### BERKONOMICS WORKBOOK
Companion to BERKONOMICS, this very personal journal contains 101 exercises for the CEO or manager that make each of the insights contained in BERKONOMICS come to life in the form of provocative and actionable questions to be answered right on the pages of the workbook. Once completed, this workbook becomes the manager's personal blueprint for business growth.

## ADVANCED BERKONOMICS
*Hard cover, soft cover and eBook editions*

Volume two of this series. One hundred and one critical insights for entrepreneurs, CEOs and board members covering the life of the company from ignition through liquidity event.   More advanced insights into planning and measurement for success with small business startups.

## SMALL BUSINESS SUCCESS SERIES
*A Series of eight short and inexpensive books or eBooks*

Take all the great material in the BERKONOMICS series and slice it by subject, and you'll have these eight inexpensive, short books about issues that you and your management team needs to focus upon today.  Ideal for giving to your entire management group for group discussions and business planning sessions.

### BOOKS and eBOOKS  IN THIS SERIES:

1. Starting Up!
2. Raising Money
3. Positioning for Success

4. Managing your Workforce
5. Protecting your Business
6. Growing your Business
7. Building Great Boards
8. Cashing Out!